Fiction 3

Series Editor: Pie Corbett

CAMBRIDGE
UNIVERSITY PRESS

CAMBRIDGE UNIVERSITY PRESS
Cambridge, New York, Melbourne, Madrid, Cape Town, Singapore, São Paulo

Cambridge University Press
The Edinburgh Building, Cambridge CB2 2RU, UK

www.cambridge.org
Information on this title: www.cambridge.org/9780521618830

© Cambridge University Press 2005

This publication is in copyright. Subject to statutory exception
and to the provisions of relevant collective licensing agreements,
no reproduction of any part may take place without the written
permission of Cambridge University Press.

First published 2005
Reprinted 2006

Printed in the United Kingdom at the University Press, Cambridge

A catalogue record for this publication is available from the British Library

ISBN-13 978-0-521-61883-0 paperback
ISBN-10 0-521-61883-5 paperback

ACKNOWLEDGEMENTS

Cover
Pulsar, Beehive Illustration

Artwork
Advocate Art (Charlotte Foulkes), Beehive Illustration (Pulsar, Sandeep Kaushik)

Texts
Familiar settings: 'The Ice Pit' by Chris Powling
Traditional tales: 'The Golden Goose' by Tony Mitton
Adventure: 'Adventure in the Spooky School' by Michaela Morgan

Contents

Familiar settings 5

'The Ice-Pit' by Chris Powling

Chapter 1 6
Chapter 2 8
Chapter 3 11
Chapter 4 14
Chapter 5 17

Traditional tales 19

'The Golden Goose' by Tony Mitton

Chapter 1 20
Chapter 2 22
Chapter 3 25
Chapter 4 27
Chapter 5 29

Adventure 33

'Adventure in the Spooky School' by Michaela Morgan

Chapter 1 34
Chapter 2 40
Chapter 3 44
Chapter 4 47
Chapter 5 51

Familiar settings

The Ice-Pit

Chapter One

Teddy was the bravest kid I ever met. He wasn't frightened of anything – not even of Haggerty Park. So why did we go there with him on that hot, summer afternoon? "We must be mad!" exclaimed Pete, my twin brother.

"Why do you say that?" Teddy asked.

"Can't you see? It's so overgrown and wild. Besides, people say there are booby traps hidden in the grass. You'll be cut in half if you step on one!"

"There's a wolf here, too," I added, nervously.

"Stories," Teddy scoffed. "Just stories."

"What about the keeper, then? He guards the place, doesn't he? Is he just a story?"

"It's Wednesday, Kit. This is his afternoon off."

"How do you know?"

"Because I've been here hundreds of times," Teddy said. "We're not going to step on a trap in broad daylight, are we? And I bet the wolf is just the keeper's Alsatian. He'll be off-duty as well. So there's nothing to be scared of, right?"

Right…

Pete and I were still worried, though. The gloom under the trees didn't look like broad daylight to us. And that rustling over in the bushes could easily have been a wolf. Anyway, where was Teddy taking us? The house itself was just a boarded-up wreck. Even the kids who told stories about Haggerty Park admitted that.

"Hey, Teddy," said Pete. "We should be at the swimming pool on a day like this."

"Good idea," I said, quickly. "Let's go back and pick up our swimming things."

"Swimming?" said Teddy.

He made it sound like doing sums. He glared at us as if he were a pirate chief facing down a mutiny.

"You really want to go swimming?" he sniffed. "When you could be having a proper adventure?"

"A proper adventure?" I gasped.

"That's right, twins!"

Teddy was beaming from ear to ear now. This made Pete and me really scared. When Teddy had that sort of look on his face, there was sure to be trouble on the way.

Chapter Two

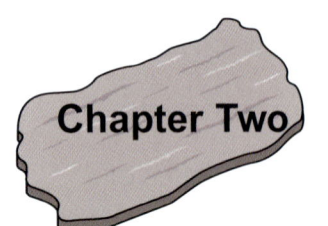

Pete and I took a look around us.

Suddenly, there seemed to be much more park than before. Of course, we knew all about its ponds and thickets and hollows. We knew all about the blackened oak tree as well. This was struck by lightning every ten years (regular as clockwork according to Teddy). We even knew about the ruined graveyard in the orchard where the family who used to live here buried their dead. Teddy himself had described these places over and over again.

In our opinion, it was dangerous enough just being in Haggerty Park. Who needed an adventure as well?

Teddy did for a start. Already he'd darted off into the woodland. "Shall we follow him?" Pete asked.

"What else can we do?" I groaned. "If we go home now, he'll never let us forget it."

So we stumbled after Teddy as quickly as we could. This wasn't easy under trees as old and twisted as these.

Especially with grass that came up to our elbows. By the time we caught up with him, he was staring across a small, shadowy clearing. "Look, twins," he pointed. "What do you think of that?"

"Depends what it is," said Pete.

"Don't you know?"

"No, I don't."

"Neither do I," I said.

Teddy looked at us as if we must be stupid. "It's an ice-pit," he said. "It's how people kept their food fresh in the olden days. Like a huge, underground fridge."

"Oh, that!" we said.

At least we'd found out where he was pointing. On the other side of the clearing was a sort of mound. This had an opening at one end. We could see a couple of stone slabs with a third slab resting across them. Between these was a dim, musty-looking gap.

"If you ask me it's prehistoric," Pete whistled.

"You reckon?" Teddy grinned.

He seemed to like the idea. It made him think of mammoths and sabre-tooth tigers, I expect. I wasn't nearly so keen. I did my best not to let this show, though. "Okay," I sniffed. "So it's an ice-pit. Who cares about that?"

"I do," said Teddy.

"I can't think why. It's only a hole in the ground. Probably it hasn't been used for ages."

"Not for storing food any more," Teddy nodded. "But it might have other uses."

"Such as what?" I asked.

Teddy frowned, thoughtfully. "A passage, maybe?" he said. "Yeah, maybe it's a passage – a secret underground passage that leads all the way to the house!"

"Or the graveyard," said Pete.

Teddy's eyes lit up at once. "Hey, I hadn't thought of that! There could be bones in there! You know, skulls and skeletons and stuff. That would be cool, wouldn't it!"

"Really cool," I managed to say. "Except we'd need ropes and torches and helmets to explore it properly."

"Yeah," Pete shuddered.

"Who's talking about exploring it properly?" Teddy said. "I only want to go in a little way…"

Chapter Three

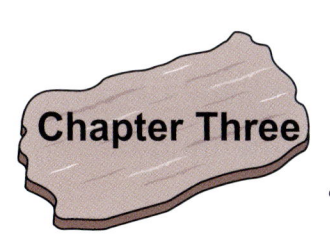

"A little way?" said Pete.

"You want us to go in there?" I said.

"Why not?" Teddy shrugged. "You don't have to come with me, twins. You can stay here as back-up."

"Back-up, Teddy?"

"In case something goes wrong, Kit."

Teddy was already on his hands and knees. He crawled into the gap between the slabs without looking back. Soon, the bit of him we could see had disappeared into the darkness. Pete and I looked at each other, white-faced. Haggerty Park was closing in. The trees, the grass, the sky … everything seemed to be nudging us towards the ice-pit.

We sighed and took a wary step forward.

Then Teddy screamed.

It was a long, jagged scream that cut through the air like a knife. It was followed by a frantic scrabbling and the thud of bone against rock. After that there was no sound at all.

Pete found his voice first. "Teddy?" he called.

"Teddy?" I joined in. "Are you okay?"

It was a stupid question, really. We already knew he wasn't. He was down there in the darkness – surrounded by skulls and skeletons. How could that be okay? Pete ran his tongue over his lips. "Kit, we'd better fetch somebody," he said.

"Not both of us, though."

"Sorry?"

"Well, we can't leave Teddy on his own. Suppose he wakes up? He'll be all alone in the ice-pit…"

"One of us must stay then."

I knew exactly what Pete was thinking. I was thinking the same thing myself. We had a difficult choice to make. Was it better to dash through Haggerty Park with its wolf and its booby-traps? Or wait here, in this dark and spooky clearing, till Teddy recovered?

Assuming he did recover, that is…

Which was worse?

It was a gust of wind that settled it. From the grass under our feet to the treetops over our heads, everything suddenly shivered. Everything, that is, except the stone slabs at the entrance to the ice-pit. "Look," I said, gritting my teeth. "I'm a couple of minutes older than you, Pete. So I'll do the choosing, okay? You keep watch over Teddy. And I'll try to fetch some help."

"The keeper will be closest, Kit."

"I know."

"Better run like mad," Pete suggested.

"And you'd better talk like mad," I told him. "Really loud, Pete. Loud enough for Teddy to hear you."

He'd already started as I turned away.

Chapter Four

I've never run so fast in my life.

I jumped over logs. I crashed through bushes. I took every short cut I could see. My feet barely touched the ground as I sprinted towards the keeper's cottage. The thought of booby-traps in the grass didn't slow me down a bit.

The wolf slowed me down, though.

It was sleeping in the keeper's front porch. Or it was till I arrived. Instantly, it pricked up its ears. I heard a growl somewhere in its throat. I saw the hair on its neck bristling. As the Alsatian slowly stood up, its pointed snout seemed to wrinkle – showing teeth that glinted in the sun. Hastily, I snatched my hand from the latch. "Mister!" I shouted. "Hey, Mister! Are you there?"

Nothing happened.

The door of the cottage stayed shut. The curtain that hung across the downstairs window didn't move. Was the keeper taking a nap in his sitting room?

Why hadn't the wolf-dog woken him up?

Because it wasn't barking, that's why. Maybe he'd trained it to snarl instead. Or maybe it always went quiet when it had the chance to attack. I realised I'd be standing there forever if I didn't attract the keeper's attention. Meanwhile, Teddy was at the bottom of the ice-pit. "Good boy!" I croaked at the Alsatian. "Good boy!"

The dog was slobbering now. Its spit lay in a bubbling puddle on the garden path. Also, it had dropped to a half-crouch. Was it about to leap over the fence and tear my throat out?

I sighed and picked up a stone.

I threw it as hard as I could at the sitting room window. Of course, it shattered at once. The jangle of breaking glass sounded like an entire greenhouse falling to bits. There were dagger-like splinters everywhere. A few of them even landed in my hair.

The keeper noticed this all right. He came hurtling out of his house in such a fury I thought for a moment he was going to leap over the fence himself and tear out my throat.

It was me making all the noise, though. "Hey, Mister!" I shrieked. "Come quickly! There's been an accident! Teddy's fallen in the ice-pit!"

"The ice-pit?" he gasped.

"Teddy might even be dead!" I wailed.

Then I burst into tears.

Chapter Five

After that the grown-ups took over. They sent two fire-tenders, an ambulance and a police car to rescue Teddy. This seemed quite a lot, really – because he wasn't even badly hurt. He had a broken arm and a headache, that's all. Being told off was far worse than the accident, he said. "Honestly, it went on for hours. I've never had such a nagging. Just about everyone had a go at me – the keeper, the police, the ambulance team. It was a right ear-bashing, I can tell you."

"What about your mum?" we asked him.

"My mum?" said Teddy.

He rolled his eyes as if he'd rather not remember what his mum said. This made Pete and me feel a bit guilty. You see, none of the grown-ups had told us off. Not even Teddy's mum. In fact, they'd treated us as if we were heroes.

Heroes?

How did they work that out? I mean, we'd been trespassing

too. Also, I'd smashed a sitting room window. As for Pete, he'd spent an hour doing nothing very much – just talking to Teddy while he lay unconscious.

What kind of heroism is that?

Of course, all this happened more than fifty years ago. Nowadays, being a grown-up myself, I can see why everyone was so pleased with Pete and me. One thing hasn't changed a bit, though. I still get a creepy feeling up and down my spine whenever I think about the ice-pit in Haggerty Park.

Traditional tales

The Golden Goose

Chapter One There was once a princess who lived as if she were under a spell. Perhaps she was, for all she would ever do was sit by the window of her tower, gazing out. Now and again she would sigh. But that was all. She would just sit there with never a smile on her face, nor a word from her lips. And no one, not even the King, her father, could get anything out of her.

The King tried everything he could think of. At first he just talked to her kindly, saying she'd be much happier if she joined in with life at court. But she hardly even looked at him. Then he told her how it was her job, as Princess, to be seen out and about more, and how he needed her help with royal duties. Still she just sat there, like someone in a dream. For all the notice she took of him, he might as well have been talking to the air.

Eventually he lost his temper. He stamped about her room in a fury, ranting and raving, saying she was a lazy, selfish, ungrateful girl who never gave a thought to anyone else. She took everything that was given to her but gave nothing in return. Still the dreamy girl just sat there, with hardly a blink. Her father could have been a fly, for all the attention she paid him.

And then the poor man broke down and cried. He knelt down by her stool and sobbed, and begged her to forgive him for getting so angry. "Will you not give me a nod or a smile, or just a glance, my daughter?"

Did she do any such thing? No. At first the King simply gave up and sat miserably on his throne. Then he began to think. Perhaps someone, somewhere, would be able to bring the Princess out of her strange mood. So he ordered a proclamation to be made. It said that if anyone could bring the Princess out of her trance, that person could marry her and rule over half the kingdom. Well, the Princess herself was very beautiful and the kingdom was large and prosperous. If that didn't encourage people, nothing would.

Chapter Two

Soon, people started to turn up at the castle. Nearly every day there was a queue which started at the gates and wound around the high walls, through the King's stables, past the guards' quarters and almost into the village. They were all waiting for their chance to make the Princess smile or laugh or say something. Each one was hoping, of course, to win the Princess as his wife, and half the kingdom with her. Some were old, some were young. Some were rich, some were poor. Some were serious, some were silly. Some were handsome, some were ugly. Some were strong, some were weak. Some were clever, some were stupid. But none were successful.

These hopeful visitors tried all sorts of things, and some of them showed wonderful skills. One man came with a whistle and played tune after tune in the King's beautiful ballroom. His first tune made the whole court weep, it was so sad. The next made them smile and laugh and chuckle, it was so full of merry mischief. Another tune filled them with fear and terror. Then the next set them dancing, it was so full of snappy rhythm. But through all this the Princess hardly stirred. It was as if the sound just couldn't reach her.

Another man came and started to clown about. At first he told jokes and funny stories. The King and his courtiers gradually got the giggles, but the Princess showed no interest. So next, he began to do funny walks in the garden outside the Princess's window. These walks got sillier and sillier until the whole court was laughing. Still the Princess showed no sign of amusement. Finally, he tried making funny faces. Some of these were so crazy that everybody was screaming with laughter. Except the Princess. She just sat there the same as ever.

Then there was the cook. He set up a small stove in the King's grand throne room and opened up a basket of fine fresh foods. He sizzled and stewed and baked and roasted. He chopped and sliced and stirred and tossed. There were savoury dishes that made nostrils quiver and mouths water. The Princess couldn't have cared less, and the lucky courtiers got to eat the food themselves. So the cook switched to making sweets and desserts – delicious delicacies to tempt one and all. The Princess barely gave them a glance. Again, the greedy courtiers did well out of the Princess's mood.

And so it went on. Whatever you can think of that might get a princess out of a trance, surer than sure, someone tried it. So in the end, people no longer came to try their luck. The word went round that it was an impossible task. The King despaired. And the Princess went on gazing in her dreamy way.

Chapter Three

Now, it happened that the castle where the King and his daughter lived stood at the top of a hill. Across the plain from this hill grew a dark, mysterious forest. And just at the edge of this forest was a simple, tumbledown cottage. This cottage was the home of Idle Jack and his poor old mother.

Idle Jack was called Idle Jack because, well, to be honest he never really did anything. He sprawled about. He lazed about. He idled. He dawdled. And that kept him busy from dawn till dusk. At least, however, he was good-natured. So, though people thought he should help his poor old mother more than he did, he was popular enough. He always had time for a smile and a laugh and a friendly word to pass the time of day.

Jack's mother kept busy. Although she was poor, the two of them had just about enough to get by on. They had a cow for milk and some chickens for eggs. To add to this, there were some fruit trees that grew around their cottage – fine trees bearing apples, pears, plums and cherries. And in the garden were plenty of vegetables. Of course, it wasn't Jack who planted them, watered them, weeded them or pulled them up when they were ready. Oh no. That was too much like hard work. He had his mother to do that for him.

But times were getting harder. The cow wasn't giving so much milk, the chickens weren't giving so many eggs, and the crop from the fruit trees was growing thinner. And as Jack's mother tilled the soil in their vegetable patch, she felt an ache in her bones that hadn't been there before. She looked at herself in their cracked mirror and said, "Hmm. I'm not getting any younger. If that boy of mine is going to make his way in the world, he'd better start shifting soon. Or when I get old and sick, he just won't know how to manage. I'd better start giving him some jobs to do. It's time he learned to work."

So, when Jack woke up earlier than usual the next day, he found his mother had drawn the curtains wide and set his boots ready beside the bed.

"Jack," she said, "you'll find a fresh loaf of bread and a bottle of good beer in your satchel. And I've sharpened our big axe. I want you to go into the forest today and chop us some firewood. Be up and off now and don't hang about. I need your help."

Chapter Four

"Well," thought Jack, "this is not what I'm used to, that's for sure. But she's been a good mother to me, and it looks like now she needs my help. I'm young and I'm strong, so I guess I can chop down an old tree or two without much trouble. Let's get on with it then."

So up he got at once. As soon as he was dressed, he slung the satchel from one shoulder, put the axe over the other, gave his old ma a kiss, and set off into the forest. "Now then, where shall I start?" he wondered. There were so many trees to choose from.

Some were too young and thin, with hardly any wood to them. Some were big and fine, but it seemed a shame to chop them down. One or two were old, but they were so huge that the task looked impossible. This woodcutting business wasn't as simple as it seemed.

It was while he was rubbing his chin and trying to choose a tree that Jack heard a voice nearby. It gave him a bit of a shock, as he'd imagined himself to be the only soul out there in the forest.

"So it's a woodcutter you're wanting to be?"

Jack turned round and was rather startled to see a wrinkled old man grinning at him from the grassy bank, just a few steps away.

"Now I'm wondering," said the old man, "if you haven't a bit of bread to spare and a wee drop of beer in that satchel of yours? I'm starved and parched as can be."

"That's just what I do have," said Jack in a good-natured way. "And you're welcome to go halves with me." So down he sat, and shared his loaf and bottle with the strange old chap.

"The tree you need is that one there," said the old man. Jack looked and saw a strange dead tree he hadn't noticed before. "That's a lucky one, I reckon," the old man added, nodding. Jack turned to ask him what he meant, but to his astonishment the old man had vanished.

"Strange," thought Jack. "Well, better get chopping."

Jack was expecting quite a hard job. Yet on the third whack of the axe, there was a flash and a crackle. The tree went tumbling down, and there, among its roots, sat a beautiful golden goose. It was alive, even though it gleamed as bright as real gold.

Chapter Five

"Amazing!" thought Jack. "It must be my lucky day. If I take this goose to the King, I bet there'll be a reward for me." So he put down his axe, tucked the goose under his arm and set off along the track to the royal castle. He hadn't been going long when he passed a cottage where a young woman stood leaning on her gate. When she saw Jack's goose, her eyes lit up.

"Oh, if I could have just one feather from that goose…" she said. And she reached out to try and pluck one. But then, lo and behold, her eager fingers stuck to the goose and she was dragged along behind Jack, unable to free herself.

"I'm off to take this goose to the King," Jack said firmly. "And nothing's going to stop me!"

The young woman began to shriek, and her sisters

came rushing out to see what the matter could be. No sooner had they patted their poor sister to help quiet her shrieking, than their hands stuck fast to her shoulders. All were pulled along behind Jack, who strode on, determined, with the goose tucked firmly under his arm.

As they passed the church, the priest came out to see what the noise was about. By now the sisters were also shrieking and the goose was cackling, but Jack strode grimly on. "You wicked women!" called the priest. "Fancy running after a young man like that! Have you no shame?" And up he went to pull them off. Of course, he too stuck fast and he too began to shout, which made him very red in the face.

Out ran the baker from the bakery, the cobbler from the shoe shop and the milkmaid from the dairy. Soon, they also were in the long, straggling line, all shrieking and wriggling, and being pulled along behind Jack, who strode on with his face set hard.

As usual, the Princess sat at her window in her trance. Then suddenly, around the bend came Jack, with the golden goose cackling under his arm and his face like thunder.

Behind Jack, wriggling and writhing and tripping and shrieking, came the whole silly, straggly line of villagers.

First the Princess smiled. Then she shook her head. Then

she giggled. And soon she was laughing helplessly. The spell was broken.

The rest is simple. The minute the spell was broken, the villagers were freed. The King got the golden goose. Jack and the Princess took to each other at once. And Jack's old ma was well looked after for the rest of her happy life.

Oh, and that little old man was neither seen nor heard of again. Fancy that!

Adventure

Adventure in the Spooky School

Chapter One

"Home at last!" sighed Jake. He pulled off his soggy coat and rubbed the rain off his glasses. It had been a long day. It had been a very, very l - o - n - g day.

Everything had gone wrong. First, he'd been told off by his teacher (for playing with the class mouse when he should have been doing his maths). Then he'd been told off by Mr Mack, the caretaker (for playing with the mouse and getting straw on the floor), and then he'd been told off AGAIN by Mr Mack (for getting straw on the floor again). "That Mr Mack really hates me," Jake muttered to himself.

Things couldn't get any worse. Then Jake's mum came in. "You did remember to bring your spellings home, didn't you?" she asked. "It's the test tomorrow."

Jake rummaged around in his bag. He found: half an apple, an old tissue, his felt-tip pen, a football sock … but no spelling book.

Wait a minute! What was that? There, snuggled up asleep in Jake's football sock, was … Click, the class mouse.

"Oh no!" Jake thought. "I must have put my spelling book in the cage – and the mouse in my bag! In the morning they'll find Click is missing and they'll know I was playing with him again. Can you imagine what they'll say? What can I do?" he wondered.

Then he had an idea. "I've forgotten my spellings, Mum!" he shouted. "But I can run back and get them."

"Be quick," his mum shouted. "It gets dark quickly at this time of year. Be back here in ten minutes."

Jake grabbed his coat and ran for the door. Now he had a choice. Should he go the sensible (but long) way? Or should he go the quick way – over the back of his garden and through the hedge into the playground?

CHOICE 1 The street way (Go to page 36.)
CHOICE 2 The quick way through the hedge (Go to page 38.)

CHOICE 1

The street way

"Better go the street way," thought Jake, and he pulled his coat on and set off. The rain was falling even more heavily now. It stung Jake's eyes. Cars swooshed past, spraying him with waves of muddy water. Rain clouds had darkened the sky until it was the strange blue-grey of a bruise.

Jake scuttled on and soon he was at his school crossing. It was then that he realised he had another problem. Normally, Jake crossed this road easily because Mr Peters, the lollipop man, popped out and held his stick firmly in the face of oncoming traffic. But there was no sign of Mr Peters – and the traffic was heavy. Swoosh, swoosh went the cars, speeding past him with their headlights glaring.

Jake stood by the road and, as he waited, he thought of all the warnings and stories he'd heard about the dangers of this road. He shivered. It seemed hopeless – he could end up standing here all night. The school lights on the other side of the road seemed to wink and mock him. Click wriggled in his bag as if to say, "Well, are you ever going to get me back?"

Then a squeal of brakes – someone had stopped for him! Headlights blinked to tell him to cross. Jake took a deep breath and ran.

CHOICE 2

The quick way through the hedge

"The hedge way is quicker," thought Jake and he grabbed his coat, dashed out of the kitchen door and across the back garden. "Gotta be quick," he said to himself, "or else Mr Mack will lock up the school."

He reached the hedge at the end of the garden. Beneath the dark, rainy sky the hedge looked like a monster crouching and ready to jump at him. "Don't be stupid!" Jake told himself but he couldn't help shivering. He scrambled along looking for the big gap that he always crawled through. "Funny!" he thought. "I was sure it was just here." But everything seemed very different under a dark sky.

He felt his way back along the hedge again.

And again.

And again.

Now he was panicking. It was getting darker and he couldn't find the gap anywhere. In the tree above him something stirred and flapped. He felt Click wriggling in his bag and knew he had to carry on – but where was that gap? Where?

It was then Jake realised that Mr Mack must have filled in the gap. He was always threatening to do that.

Yes! Now Jake could see a panel of shining metal. The metal glinted. There was only the smallest gap left. Jake gritted his teeth and pushed his way through the tiny gap. Branches tore at him, twigs scratched him, but he made it. Jake took a deep breath and ran towards the school entrance.

Chapter Two

Jake felt hot and damp and breathless. The journey to school had taken much, much longer than it should have done and now it was really beginning to get dark. There was a rumble of thunder.

He crept into the silent school. This was the same old school that he went to every day of the week. It was a two-storey building surrounded by a playground on one side and a field with trees on the other side. The field led to the back of the row of houses where Jake lived. Every day of his life Jake had looked at this building. It was as familiar to him as his own house but now, in the growing dark and the quiet, everything seemed strange. Behind him a door creaked in the wind.

In the distance he could hear something. Was it Mr Mack? Jake's heart pounded. If Mr Mack found him here, with the mouse, there'd be trouble again. He had to get Click back to the classroom – without Mr Mack seeing him. But how?

He could creep through the cloakrooms. The lights were off in the cloakrooms and Jake could sneak through the shadows – but the cloakrooms looked so strange in the half-dark. Jake shivered at the thought of going through there. He could go straight across the hall – but then he might meet Mr Mack.

What should he do?

CHOICE 1 The cloakrooms (Go to page 42.)
CHOICE 2 The hall (Go to page 43.)

CHOICE 1

The cloakrooms

"Safer to go through the cloakrooms," Jake decided, and he started to creep through the first of the littered cloakrooms on his way to his classroom. The cloakrooms were narrow, small, windowless rooms and Jake was too afraid of being spotted to switch on the lights. The hall lights were still on so he could dimly see, but it was a world of shadows he was now creeping through. Abandoned socks were curled up like rats ready to leap at him, a forgotten coat hanging on a hook looked like a headless man…

It was with a sigh of relief that he arrived at the classroom door.

CHOICE 2
The hall

"Quicker to go straight through the hall," Jake decided. But then as he peered around the door into the hall he felt as vulnerable as a field mouse about to scuttle over an open field – while above him a huge owl-like Mr Mack was circling ready to pounce. He took a deep breath and made a run for it. His movements made Class Three's mobiles sway back and forth and cast twisted shadows on the floor. His own footsteps had never sounded so noisy. They seemed to echo all around him in that big, hollow space with its dark corners. Mr Mack would surely hear and come running to investigate!

Jake slid to a stop at the other side of the hall and sighed with relief, "Made it!"

Chapter Three

Jake's hand shook as he opened his classroom door. He'd never been in his class in the dark before. He crept around in the shadows. Wall displays loomed at him. One wall was covered in portraits of the class and the eyes of every portrait seemed to be staring straight at Jake. In the corner a tap dripped. Drip. Drip. Drip. It was a sad, quiet sound. He could see Click's cage, its metal bars glinting like a monster's teeth.

Jake felt around in his bag, found Click and popped him into the cage. Then he grabbed his spelling book, but before Jake had a chance to close the catch on the cage door, he froze. He had heard something! There were footsteps. Footsteps in the distance – and they were coming closer.

He had to hide – but where? Should he just crouch under the teacher's desk and hope no one would see him? Or should he go into the dark store cupboard? There was no way anyone would spot him in there – but it looked so dark. And what if he got locked in? Where should he hide?

CHOICE 1 Hide under desk (Go to page 45.)

CHOICE 2 Hide in cupboard (Go to page 46.)

CHOICE 1

Hide under desk

Quick as a rat, Jake slipped under the teacher's desk and crouched there trying to keep still, trying to hold his breath. The bin in front of him was stuffed with scraps of paper and pencil shavings and Jake suddenly realised that Mr Mack might be coming to empty it. If Mr Mack moved the bin he would find Jake straightaway! The footsteps were getting louder and louder. They were definitely coming towards him.

 Jake was stiff with fear. What would Mr Mack say if he discovered him here? The classroom door squeaked open wider. Jake peered out from his hiding place and saw a pair of trainers and a pair of ripped jeans coming towards him. "Ripped jeans on Mr Mack!" he thought. "Funny!" And then another pair of legs came in and Jake realised it wasn't Mr Mack coming into the classroom at all. Who were these mysterious intruders?

CHOICE 2

Hide in cupboard

Jake dived into the store cupboard but kept the door ajar. Shelves stuffed with paper, books and pots of paint surrounded him. The cupboard smelt of old pencil shavings and glue.

From one shelf, something long and white reached towards him. It was a bony arm! Jake stifled his scream. "It's only the paper skeleton!" he told himself. (It was part of last term's work on The Human Body.) But he couldn't help stepping back from it – and as he stepped back he leant against something sticky and clammy. It was only sponges and paint, but he wanted to run shouting and screaming from the cupboard. He couldn't do that – the footsteps were coming closer and closer.

Chapter Four

The footsteps came to a stop. The mysterious intruders were whispering to each other now. Jake could hear them heaving heavy objects. He peered out cautiously. They were taking the class computers.

"There's another one over there," the girl whispered, "and a telly and a video out in the hall."

"Get a move on then," the boy hissed. "And keep it quiet. We don't want that caretaker finding us."

They must be burglars! And they were within inches of him. Jake held his breath. They would definitely find him! Suddenly there was a scuttling sound. Jake knew exactly what it was. He hadn't closed the cage firmly and Click was out and about again. The sudden noise and movement briefly startled the two burglars. They both jumped and turned around – and that gave Jake the chance to get away.

He was out of his hiding place and running, running as fast as his legs would carry him. Had the burglars spotted him? Were they after him? Jake looked around in a panic. Which way should he go?

The stairs were just in front of him. If he went that way he'd get to the Head's office in seconds. Then he could phone the police. But what if the burglars followed him? There was no way to get out of the school from up there. What if he ran down the corridor to the Secretary's office? It was much further away but she had a phone too – and the way out of school was just next to her office.

CHOICE 1 The stairs (Go to page 49.)
CHOICE 2 The corridor (Go to page 50.)

CHOICE 1
The stairs

Jake ran up the stairs two at a time. His heart was pounding and his throat burning. He took the turn on the stairs by grabbing onto the banister and swinging himself around. If Mr Mack or his headteacher had seen him Jake knew what they would say: "NO RUNNING ON THE STAIRS! YOU KNOW IT'S DANGEROUS!" They could have no idea how dangerous it was now. If he lost his footing he would fall – and be found by the burglars. What would they do to him?

He reached the top of the stairs, gasping. Down at the bottom of the corridor was the Head's office, and a phone. He would phone the police and hope they were quick. And he would hope against hope that the Head's office was not locked.

CHOICE 2

The corridor

"Much better to run towards the outside world, even if it is longer," Jake decided and he set off sprinting down the corridor. Never had a corridor looked so long and so straight! There were no hiding places – the burglars could clearly see him if they were following him. He turned round. He couldn't see them following him – yet.

Jake panted and gasped. His heart thumped and his legs felt far too shaky to run but he pounded on down the corridor. He was getting closer and closer to the Secretary's office and the door to the outside world. He prayed that both doors were still unlocked.

Chapter Five

With his heart racing inside his chest, Jake reached the office. It was unlocked! The phone was on the desk by the window. He knew what to do. All he had to do was phone 999. But would they believe him?

And what was that sound – was that the burglars coming towards him? Out of the window Jake could see something else – Mr Mack! The caretaker was walking back from the hedge carrying a bag of litter and grumbling to himself. Jake could just call out of the window to Mr Mack. That would be quick but the burglars would hear him. Jake felt dizzy and sick. He didn't know what was the best thing to do.

CHOICE 1 Phone the police (Go to page 52.)

CHOICE 2 Call out of the window to the caretaker (Go to page 54.)

CHOICE 1
Phone the police

With a shaky hand, Jake picked up the phone and dialled 999.

"Emergency. Which service do you require?" asked the operator.

"Police!" Jake gasped. "Quick! There are…"

"Name and telephone number?" asked the operator.

"J-J-Jake Thomas, 225498," Jake stammered. "There are…"

"Transferring you now," said the operator.

Jake's knees were beginning to buckle under him. This was all TOO

SLOW. They were going to get him. They were going to get him.

"Police," said another voice.

"You've got to be quick!" Jake whispered. "Please. They're going to…"

"Take your time and speak clearly please…" the voice continued.

Jake was in despair. Surely those were footsteps he could hear coming down the corridor? It was too late. He was doomed.

Go to page 56.

CHOICE 2

Call out of the window to the caretaker

Jake decided it was worth taking the chance. He rapped on the window and waved frantically. A startled Mr Mack looked up at him. Jake pushed the window open. "Help!" Jake hissed. "Burglars in the school. They're…"

Mr Mack looked surprised for a moment, then gestured towards the school gate, saying in a loud whisper, "I'll go and get help."

Jake would have expected him to rush out, but with dismay he saw the caretaker turn away and walk out of the school gate, oh, so slowly. He was still carrying the sack of litter.

"Doesn't he realise it's an emergency?" Jake groaned. "Now I'm stuck. All alone. And the burglars might have heard me calling from the window." In fact, he thought he could hear them now. Jake felt like a rabbit frozen in a car's headlights. All he could do was wait for the disaster to happen…

Go to page 56.

Chapter Five (continued)

Jake stayed very still and listened.

He heard voices shouting.

He heard footsteps running.

He heard a CRASH.

And then the door to the office opened.

Jake held his breath and gazed at the floor. Two pairs of shiny black boots and one pair of squishy old trainers were coming towards him. He raised his eyes and, to his relief, saw that the boots belonged to a policeman and a policewoman and the trainers belonged to Mr Mack. Jake had never been so glad to see Mr Mack before. "I had to come back for … my spellings," he said, "and I heard these burglars, so…"

"It's all right, you did the right thing," said Mr Mack.

The policewoman was reassuring. "Well done! If it hadn't been for you, we would never have caught them so quickly," she said. "Come on. We'll take you home now."

"I'll lock up," said Mr Mack, "but first I have to catch that pesky mouse. He's out of the cage again. How does he do it?"